The Folly of Atheism

"The fool hath said in his heart:
'There is no God'."
(Psalm 14 verse 1)

Fraser A. Munro

Introduction

Geoffrey Bull was a British missionary in Tibet in the early 1950s. He was captured by Chinese Communists and held prisoner by them for three long years. He was then released and he travelled widely, telling his story.

During his imprisonment, the Chinese authorities tried to indoctrinate him. They wanted to see him 'converted' from Christianity to Communism. He describes in one of his books - *'When Iron Gates Yield'* - how he was given books to read. In one such book, the author 'paraded evolutionary theory as fact' and concluded his writing with a prediction that Communism would triumph, that a Communist state would be established, that classes would be eliminated and that religious faith would disappear.

Mr Bull also had to listen to Communist propaganda. He describes one occasion when for 20 hours, men raged at him on the question of evolution. In his own words: 'The Marxist development of the teaching of Darwin is the very core of their atheistic social concepts'.

Now, to paint another picture and to sketch another scene, two head teachers permit the distribution of books at their school and such is the backlash that they are removed from their posts and redeployed. What sinister books were these? What awful things did they contain? One was called *'How Do You Know God is Real?'* and the other was called *'Exposing the Myth of Evolution'*.

Another case involves a physics class discussion on the Big Bang. The teacher expressed the view that evolution had not been proved. Again there was a reaction - and a result. For the six months until the teacher retires, he is to be 'monitored' and his classes will be taught by someone else. In the Press, a suggestion has been expressed that those with creationist views should not be allowed to teach.

Where were these incidents set? Where is it that 'evolutionary theories are being paraded as fact'? Where is it that to get and keep a particular job, a Christian might decide to be circumspect in declaring his faith? Where is it that prospective adopters, wanting to welcome a child into their family, might need to be careful in what they say about what they believe?

Not Communist China in the early 1950s, but secular Scotland in 2013!

For years, the reaction to the Gospel in Scotland has largely been that of apathy. Now, in many quarters, the reaction is hostility. Atheism is growing louder in its voice and stronger in its force. The latest Census result disclosed that 37% of people in Scotland declare that they have no religious belief, an increase of 9% in 10 years.

Well may we speak about 'the ferocity of atheism'!

When we come to *Psalm 14 verse 1*, however, we see something different. It is not the ferocity of atheism, but the *folly* of atheism. Declares the Psalmist: "The fool hath said in his heart: 'There is no God'." So important is this point that this verse is one of the repeated verses in the Bible. We find it here and then we find it again in *Psalm 53 verse 1*. So essential is this truth that God deems it essential to speak it twice!

Can I suggest that we can speak about **the Sevenfold Folly of Atheism**? There are seven reasons why the atheist is foolish.

Firstly, Atheism is foolish because atheism ignores creation around us.

You visit a home and enter the study. On the desk you see a globe. The countries and continents of the world are all named. The oceans of the world are all coloured in blue. The globe itself rests on a brass stand.

On the globe, there is no date of manufacture, but no-one would deny its manufacture. To do so would be absurd! The globe exists and there must have been a cause for its existence. The globe cannot exist uncaused and it must owe its existence to something or someone outside of itself.

This is elementary! Anything with a beginning must have a beginner. Anything with an origin must have an originator.

If this is true about a representation of the world, then it must be equally true, it must be even more true, of the real world.

The existence of a painting demands the existence of a painter. The existence of a sculpture demands the existence of a sculptor. The existence of a book demands the existence of an author. The existence of creation demands the existence of a creator.

To say, as many do, that men came from monkeys, that monkeys came from lower beasts, that lower beasts came from slime, that slime came from water on the earth, that the earth came from complex gases that collided in a Big Bang, and that complex gases came from primitive gases is inadequate. Even were that explanation all correct, (which we deny), those who offer that explanation would need to answer: And from where did the primitive gases come?

Atheism cannot answer the argument from *cause* - and atheism cannot answer the argument from *design*.

Centuries ago, there lived a man called William Paley.

He imagined himself walking across a heath and seeing and finding a watch. If he examined it and saw how it was constructed and how it worked, he would see in it clear evidence of design and deduce from it that there had been a designer. It would be illogical to conclude that it was the result of blind forces. Time, matter and chance could never have combined to produce it - not even after the passing of the longest of Ages.

In creation, there is evidence of design. Evidence of intelligent design! A telescope reveals the immensity of creation. A microscope reveals the intricacy of creation. Even a single cell is incredibly complex. We now know that every cell has its own genetic code. Here is Professor John Lennox: 'Every one of the 10 to 100 trillion cells in the human body contains a database larger than the *"Encyclopaedia Britannica"*.'[1]

If I enter a town and see a sign: 'Kilmarnock. This is Wallace Country. The Creative Place', do I suppose that those letters appeared by chance? No! It would be obvious that they were there by design, by intent, by purpose. If that is true of a sign with three short statements, what will we say about an individual cell containing more information than a whole collection of books?

Wherever we look, we see evidence of design! The universe, the earth, the human body, all finely tuned to support life. Wherever we look, we see evidence of a designer!

So much is said about evolution, but it has been said - by Dr Bert Cargill, a retired science lecturer with a first class honours degree in chemistry - that there are **'10 Things About Evolution that We are Not Often Told'**:

Number 1: Evolution is not a fact.
It is a theory, based on some facts, much speculation, many assumptions - and it has never been proved.

Number 2: Evolution is not probable - likely to happen - nor reasonable - making good sense.
The odds against the main components of it are huge.

Number 3: Evolution is not supported by the fossil record.
There are no simple fossils at start.
There are no 'link' fossils 'between'.

Number 4: It is not certain that the world is thousands of millions of years old.
That age is calculated on the basis of assumptions unlikely to be true.

Number 5: Energy - which fills the universe - cannot be created by nothing and from nothing.
This is a statement of a law of science to which no exception exists in the real world.

Number 6: Complex structures (e.g. protein molecules, cells) do not by themselves come from simpler ones.

This is a statement of another law of science with no exceptions.

This law - and experience - says that complex structures rather break down into simpler ones by themselves – and that chaos and disorder happen in systems when left to themselves.

Number 7: Life does not come from non-living matter. This is also a law of science - the law of biogenesis - always obeyed in the real world.

Number 8: Many scientists do not believe in evolution. Among them are some scientists with no religious faith, with no belief in God.

Number 9: People do believe in evolution because they do not want to believe in God.

Number 10: The Bible is not contradicted by any fact of science.
The Book of Spiritual Revelation and the Book of Nature have the same Author, so they must agree – and they do. Biology, chemistry, physics, astronomy, archaeology are all sciences which have provided data which are not at odds with what the Bible says.

Says our Psalmist, this time in *Psalm 19*: 'The Heavens declare the glory of God, the firmament sheweth His handiwork'. When an atheist declared he was going to remove every reference to God, someone replied: 'Begin, then, by taking down the stars!' 'In the stars, His handiwork I see!'

Says Paul in *Romans 1*: 'The invisible things of Him from the creation of the world are clearly seen'. Fred Stallan, in his commentary on *Romans,* observes: 'Creation is not dumb!' It has spoken long - from creation's day. It has spoken loud - 'clearly seen'.

Wherever we look, at whatever we look, labels as it were that say: 'Made in Heaven' and 'Made by God'.

Is there no God? The stream that silver flows
The air he breathes, the ground he treads, the trees,
The flowers, the grass, the sand, each wind that blows,
All speak of God; throughout, one voice agrees,
And, eloquent, His dread existence shows -
Blind to thyself, ah, see Him, fool, in these![2]

Atheism is foolish because atheism ignores creation around us.

Secondly, Atheism is foolish because atheism ignores conscience within us.

Remember the story of *John 8*! The woman taken in adultery! The religious leaders bring her to the Lord. 'Moses commanded us that such should be stoned: but what sayest Thou?'

A cunning plan, they thought, to trap Christ. If He said:

'Let her die!', then He would be in conflict with Rome. If He said: 'Let her live!', then He would be in conflict with Moses. If He pronounced 'Death!' - where was His mercy? If He pronounced 'Life!' - where was His justice?

Thus they challenged Him - and then He challenged them. 'He that is without sin among you, let him first cast a stone at her.'

John records: 'They which heard it, being convicted by their own conscience, went out one by one, beginning at the eldest, even unto the last'. The accusers are themselves accused. The judges are themselves judged. The condemners are themselves condemned.

They display a common reaction. They all do the same thing - they all walk away, but it would not be true to call it a collective reaction. Individually, independently, inwardly, each is convicted by his own conscience. Then we read: 'And Jesus was left alone'. That was significant! The only man with a clear conscience. The only man with a sinless soul.

Romans 2 speaks about: 'The work of the law written in their hearts' and 'conscience bearing witness' and 'thoughts accusing or else excusing'. We ask the question: 'Who wrote the law in the hearts of men?' The answer is: 'God!' We ask the question: 'From where did man get his conscience?' The answer is: 'From God!'

Conscience - God's messenger in each heart! Conscience - God's deputy in each soul. That instinctive, inherent awareness of the difference between what is good and what is bad, between what is right and what is wrong.

Man is more than chemical compounds. Within us all, a conscience that says, that cries: 'I ought' or 'I ought not'. Within us all, a conscience that convicts, that produces shame and a sense of guilt when I do not heed its voice.

Man is a moral creature. He has a moral appreciation. He has a moral standard. He has a moral compass.

It is that sense of morality that causes the atheist to play, what he thinks is, his trump card, to pose, what he thinks is, his hardest question, to present, what he thinks is, his strongest argument: 'If God exists, why does evil exist?'

That was the suggestion made to Ravi Zacharias at a university down south. 'There cannot possibly be a God,' the student said, 'with all the evil, all the suffering in the world!' Mr Zacharias responded: 'When you say there is such a thing as evil, are you not assuming that there's such a thing as good?' 'Of course!', the student retorted. 'But when you assume there's such a thing as good - are you not assuming there's a moral law on the basis of which to distinguish between good and evil?' 'I suppose so!' came the hesitant and much softer reply.

'If then', said Zacharias, 'there is a moral law, then you must accept there's a moral law-giver. But, that's who you are trying to disprove! If there is no transcendent moral law-giver, then there is no absolute moral law. If there is no moral law, there really is no good. If there is no good, there is no evil - and I am not sure what your question is!' There was silence and then the student spoke: 'What, then, am I asking you?' and sheepishly sat down.[3]

If there is no objective moral standard, then who are we to say that anything is wrong?

An atheist in a debate tried to argue that morality was determined by society. That is, perhaps, a common view. Whatever the majority think, stands as the standard. 'So', replied a Christian, 'in Nazi Germany, you would have to say that there was nothing wrong about killing six million Jews?' The atheist paused and then, maintaining his position, said: 'Yes! There was nothing wrong in that!' Beside him, however, in the lecture hall sat his friend, another atheist. He cried out, indeed he felt compelled to cry out: 'No!' He was right to object, right to intervene, right to cry out. He was aware of the moral law, placed in his heart by the law-giver.

The existence of evil does not contradict the existence of God. Our acknowledgement that some things are evil and our acknowledgement that evil exists confirms the existence of God, the moral law-giver.

So atheism is foolish because atheism ignores conscience within us.

Thirdly, Atheism is foolish because atheism ignores cravings from us.

Man is a moral creature, but man is more than that. Man is a religious creature. Man is a spiritual creature.

He has a longing for fulfilment. He has an urge to worship. He has a tendency to turn to God in trouble. You know the saying: 'There are no atheists in the trenches'. He has a craving for eternity.

Remember Solomon! Solomon - the Preacher. Solomon - the Searcher. His exercise in *Ecclesiastes* is to search for purpose in life, to explore the meaning of life, to secure satisfaction from life. Viewed through natural reasoning, viewed in the sphere 'under the sun', life seems pointless and profitless, unfair and unfulfilling. The experiences of life do not satisfy his heart. The events of life do not satisfy his mind.

Then, he recognises a spiritual dimension: God has 'made everything beautiful in his time. He hath set the world (eternity, an awareness of eternity) in their heart' (Chapter 3 verse 11). The heart of man is too big to be filled with all the pleasures and possessions of earth. In the well-known words: 'There is a God-shaped void that only He can fill!'[4]

Man was made by God's hand, made in God's image, made after God's likeness and made for God's company. Into man, God breathed!

Here is C. S. Lewis: 'Creatures are not born with desires - unless satisfaction for those desires exists. A baby feels hunger - well, there is such a thing as food. A duckling wants to swim - well, there is such a thing as water. If I find in myself a desire which no experience in this world can satisfy, the most probable explanation is that I was made for another world'.[5]

Atheism is foolish because atheism ignores the cravings from us.

Fourthly, Atheism is foolish because atheism ignores the care upon us.

We are in *Acts 14*. We are at Lystra. We are listening to the Apostle Paul: God 'left not Himself without witness'. This is God's witness to Himself. This is God's evidence of Himself. 'He did good and gave us rain from Heaven and fruitful seasons, filling our hearts with food and gladness'. The truth of divine providence! The truth of common grace!

Says the hymn writer:
> 'Summer and winter and spring-time and harvest,
> Sun, moon and stars in their courses above,
> Join with all nature in manifold witness,
> To Thy great faithfulness, mercy and love'.

The good God does! The gifts God sends! His power! His patience - even when men went astray! Says Matthew Henry: 'His goodness is His glory!' How good that He fills our hearts with food and joy! Humanity's great Benefactor! Humanity's great Philanthropist!

Atheism is foolish because atheism ignores the care upon us.

Fifthly, Atheism is foolish because atheism ignores the Canon of Scripture before us.

Read the Bible and hundreds of times you will read the words 'Thus saith the Lord'. On that basis, for that reason, we can say that the Bible contains the words of God. But more can be said! Not only does the Bible contain the words of God, it *is* the Word of God. From *Genesis 1 verse 1* to *Revelation 22 verse 21*, it was given by inspiration of God. All is God-breathed. Every book, every chapter, every verse, every word, every syllable, every letter - has come from God.

Stamped upon its pages are distinctive characteristics, divine characteristics that show that the Bible is God's Word.

Think of its Authenticity.
It is an ancient Book, but an ancient Book that has been accurately preserved. Although no original manuscripts exist, literally thousands of fragments of copies, dating

back centuries, do exist. We can be quite confident that what we now read is what was then written.

Think of its Harmony.
If any book had been commenced 1500 years before it concluded, then at best, revision, and at worst, rejection, but not this Book. When the books of the Bible are put together, they fit together. There is no discrepancy. There is no contradiction. They form a complete whole and the explanation is easy. Behind the forty individual writers is one single Author - God Himself.

Think of its Prophecy.
It has been said that 30% of the Bible is prophecy. There are any number of explicit predictions, many of which have already been exactly fulfilled. Hundreds of predictions have been fulfilled to the very letter and often by people with no knowledge of them and no interest in them. All this is an absolute impossibility in terms of chance, but again the explanation is easy. The prophecies come from God. He inhabits eternity. All things - past, present and future - are known to Him.

Think of its Accuracy.
Over the centuries, men have made discoveries in the realms of geography and history and archaeology and no discovery, in any realm, has ever uncovered any mistake.

Think of its Inexhaustibility.
No matter how often we read it and no matter how well

we think we know it, when we come to the Bible afresh, we find something fresh. Said C. H. Spurgeon: 'The Bible is always a new Book. There is not a stale page in the Word of God. It is just as fresh as though the ink were not yet dry'.[6]

Think of its Beauty.
The story is told of a day when people were discouraged from reading the Bible by their so-called religious leaders. At such a time, there was a man who spent his days going from home to home, offering Bibles for sale. He arrived at one house. The door was opened by a young woman. He explained his purpose. 'Would she like a Bible?' She was very dismissive. 'Oh!' she said, 'The Bible's a bad book. The devil wrote it!' The man replied: 'Let me read from it and you can judge who wrote it'. He turned to *John 14* and read these words: 'Let not your heart be troubled. Ye believe in God, believe also in Me. In My Father's house are many mansions. If it were not so, I would have told you. I go to prepare a place for you'. He then read further down the chapter: 'Peace I leave with you. My peace I give unto you. Let not your heart be troubled, neither let it be afraid'. The man looked up and asked his question: 'Who wrote it?' With tears in her eyes, the lady replied: 'This Book has come from Heaven! This Book was written by God!' There is a beauty about the Bible unsurpassed, unequalled by any other book.

Think of its Invincibility.
For any book to survive for centuries is remarkable. For

this Book to have survived for centuries is most remarkable! It has been the object of the most immense, intense attack. Men and groups of men, societies and systems, have sought to destroy the Bible. They have endeavoured to remove it from the face of the earth. However, these attempts have always failed. It is indestructible. It is invincible. It is nothing short of a miracle that we have a copy of the Bible today.

These are the Bible's distinctive characteristics and now these are the Bible's delightful contents. It has been well said:

'This Book contains the mind of God; the state of man; the way of salvation; the doom of sinners and the happiness of believers ... Read it to be wise; believe it to be safe, and practise it to be holy ... It contains light to direct you; food to support you and comfort to cheer you ... It is the traveller's map; the pilgrim's staff; the pilot's compass; the soldier's sword and the Christian's charter'.

John Wesley wrote: 'I am a creature of a day, passing through life as an arrow through the air. I am a spirit come from God and returning to God; just hovering over the great gulf till, a few moments hence, I am no more seen. I drop into an unchangeable eternity. I want to know one thing - the way to Heaven; how to land safe on that happy shore. God Himself has condescended to teach me the way. He hath written it down in a Book. O, give me that Book! At any price, give me the Book of

God! I have it. Here is knowledge enough for me. Let me be *homo unius libri*. A man of one Book!'[7]

Atheism is foolish because atheism ignores the Canon of Scripture before us.

Sixthly, Atheism is foolish because atheism ignores the Christ who came to us.

A man who lived a short life! Long ago! Far away! Most of His life was spent in obscurity. All of his life was spent in poverty. His life ends in ignominy. He dies young - upon a Cross and forsaken by his followers.

And yet! He changed earth's chronology. We now speak about B.C. and A.D. He changed earth's history. He is the supreme personality, the most dominant figure of all time.

It has been pointed out that He never wrote a book. He never painted a picture. He never composed a song. However, more books have been written about Him and more paintings painted of Him and more songs have been composed in His honour than that of anyone else. We today and so many around the world take to ourselves His name and call ourselves - Christians.

Says John Blanchard: 'Jesus Christ presents an enormous problem for the atheist!'[8] An enormous problem, for attention is drawn to this man. At His birth - the star and the seraph and the Shekinah glory and the swaddling bands. In His life - messages from heaven and miracles on earth. At His death - strange darkness, the rent veil, the quaking of rocks and open graves. He had a unique birth, a unique life and a unique death.

He dies but that is not the end. The tomb was empty. His grave-clothes are left behind. Reports of the Risen Christ come from women and men; from individuals and couples, and from small companies and large crowds. People who were expecting Him to appear and people who doubted that He would appear - saw Him.

Disciples characterised by fear when Christ dies become emboldened days later. They spend their lives preaching the Gospel and many then give their lives in defence of the Gospel. A transformation from cowardice to courage and the only explanation must be that what they *said* was true *was* in fact true.

C. S. Lewis had his great trilemma. (A dilemma is a choice between two options and a trilemma is a choice between three options.). Said Lewis of Christ - the options are these. The first is that He is a liar - a man who deliberately made false claims. Could that be true? The second is that He is a lunatic - a man who deludedly made false claims. Could that be true? That leaves only the third option - He is Lord.[9]

The evidence compels us to agree with the message of Scripture: 'God who at sundry times and in divers manners, spake in time past unto the fathers by the prophets, hath in these last days spoken unto us by His Son'. That is *Hebrews 1*.

'No man hath seen God at any time. The only begotten Son which is in the bosom of the Father, He hath declared Him'. That is *John 1*!

'Show us the Father', says Philip in the upper room, 'and that will be enough for us'. Jesus said: 'He that hath seen Me hath seen the Father'.

It was blessedly possible to turn the corner of the street in Israel in those days and come face-to-face with God manifest in the flesh. 'The glory of God in the face of Jesus Christ!'

God has been here! Ours is the visited planet.

Atheism is foolish because atheism ignores the Christ who came to us.

Seventhly, Atheism is foolish because atheism ignores conversions among us.

In *Acts 4*, the religious leaders have a problem. They were indignant at the preaching of Christ by the apostles and yet they were impotent, for standing with the believers was a man who had been healed. Says Luke: 'They could say nothing against it'. Said the leaders themselves: 'That indeed a notable miracle hath been done ... is manifest to all ... and we cannot deny it'.

The powerful testimony, the powerful evidence and the powerful witness of a changed life!

His is but one of many changed lives in *Acts*. Men at Jerusalem who had rejected Christ, received Him. Saul of Tarsus, the enemy of the Cross becomes the evangelist of the Cross. The persecutor becomes the preacher. The Philippian jailer - stripes inflicted upon his prisoners and then stripes washed.

Acts ends in that most significant way with Paul preaching and teaching concerning the Lord Jesus Christ. Preaching and continuing to preach, preaching and no record of any conclusion, for in a sense the story of *Acts* has never come to a close.

The Lord Jesus continues to be preached. He continues to be presented and over the long centuries, the most unlikely of individuals and the vilest of offenders have come to this Book, read its pages, understood its message, bowed to its claims and trusted in the Christ - and undergone a remarkable and miraculous transformation into the sweetest of saints.

Matthew Parris, *'The Times'* journalist and himself an atheist has said this: 'In Africa Christianity changes people's hearts. It brings a spiritual transformation. The rebirth is real. The change is good'.[10]

So despite the fact that around us today in increasing numbers and with interesting volume the cry is heard, the assertion is made and the claim is presented: **'There is no God!'**, those who so speak are fools. They are guilty of the greatest and the gravest folly.

They are fools because atheism ignores –

> *Creation around us,*
> *Conscience within us,*
> *Cravings from us,*
> *Care upon us,*
> *The Canon before us,*
> *The Christ who came to us, and*
> *The Conversions around us.*

The Christian has no reason whatsoever to be ashamed of his faith!

Our Psalm concludes, in verse 7:

'Oh that the salvation of Israel were come out of Zion! When the Lord bringeth back the captivity of His people, Jacob shall rejoice, and Israel shall be glad'.

Says Spurgeon: 'Natural enough is this closing prayer for what would so effectively convince atheists, overthrow persecutors, stay sin and secure the godly as the manifest appearance of Israel's great Salvation.'

Says Spurgeon: 'O that these weary years would have an end! O that He were come! What happy, holy, halcyon, heavenly days should we then see! Blessed are all they that wait for Him!'

---

[1] *God's Undertaker - Has Science Buried God?* by John Lennox, p.128.
[2] Poem by Giovanni Cotta quoted by CH Spurgeon in *The Treasury of David*.
[3] Story in *Can Man Live Without God?* by Ravi Zacharias.
[4] Quote from Blaise Pascal.
[5] *Mere Christianity* by CS Lewis.
[6] From a sermon preached on 15th April 1869.
[7] John Wesley's Preface to *Sermons on Several Occasions*.
[8] *Does God Believe in Atheists?* by John Blanchard.
[9] *Mere Christianity* by CS Lewis.
[10] *The Times*, 27th December 2008.